Managing Students Through Relationships NOT Rules

Glenn P. Brooks, Jr.

Glenn P. Brooks, Jr.

Managing Students Through Relationships NOT Rules

Copyright ©2015
Glenn P. Brooks, Jr. LLC

All rights reserved.

No part of this publication may be reproduced, stored in a retrieval system, or transmitted in any form or by any means (electronic, mechanical, photocopying, recorded, or otherwise) without prior written permission.

ISBN-13:
978-1514617342

ISBN-10:
151461734X

Printed in the United States of America

Cover design by Vexed Graphics

For more information visit
www.GlennPBrooksJr.com

Table of Contents

Introduction 7

Rules – Relationships = Rules 15

It's all in a name 27

Atta boy! 35

What you see is what you get 47

Give honor where it is due 57

Perception is reality 67

Caring starts with us 73

See what you see 81

Always be there 89

Notes 97

Acknowledgments 99

About the author 101

Introduction

At a very challenging point in my life I was faced with making a huge decision that quite frankly I had been avoiding for a number of years. What was the huge decision? It was how was I going to make a career change so that it would enable me to better provide for my family? I was no stranger to working hard, but in 2006 when I along with an entire team and our families relocated to Georgia from Maryland I had no idea of the direction that it would take me and my family. We had no idea how difficult it would be to establish a non-profit outreach to a community that had just began to experience one of the toughest economic down turns that our nation had seen in quite some time.

Most of my adult life I have been involved in the people business in one form or another. From my days in the Army, to radio, and then later in ministry working with students and adults I have been a part of building leadership teams in both the public and private sector of the work force, including for profit and non-profit industries. After almost fourteen years working for a non-profit organization I was faced with having to make a transition in my career in order to better provide for my family. The downturn in the economy had caused major strain on the organization and my family personally so I had to decide the course for this next chapter of my life. I could have chosen to go back to radio but that is not where my heart was. So when researching my options on what was next, I took into consideration my particular skill set and passion. I needed to find something that could incorporate my gift of connecting with people, building teams, public speaking and inspiring others. Ultimately it was my desire to continue to do something that would make a difference and not merely collect a paycheck.

Then it came to me… How about driving a school bus? For the past few months I had noticed billboards and signage on school buses throughout Gwinnett County regarding the need for school bus drivers. Having worked as a mentor, youth leader, and summer camp director I was passionate about working with children of all ages and it made sense. I had a heart for children so this was a great opportunity which would also provide me with a steady pay check and have the summers off with pay "woo-hoo." I stepped down from my positon at the non-profit and started a new adventure as a Bus Manager with Gwinnett County public schools.

It was the perfect transition for a guy that had spent years working in the lives of students. I quickly learned that one of, if not the most difficult jobs for a bus manager was managing the behavior of elementary, middle and high school students. This was coupled with having somewhere between forty-eight and seventy-two students at one time per route for regular education bus drivers. In conjunction with driving a big yellow metal can in rush hour traffic in the early morning and late afternoon. Then throw in a little inclement weather and you have the makings of what can be an incredibly stressful work environment. Although, special needs drivers transport fewer students they have the additional responsibility of managing students that have emotional, psychological and physical special needs along with the above challenges.

This can be a challenge for the rookie or veteran driver. Managing students successfully is something that requires patience, persistence and passion. It also is a skill set that can be learned. But make no mistake it requires having a true "heart" for children.

I have had the pleasure of serving and working in the lives of students and parents for over twenty-five years and I am constantly learning new methods for managing students. My hope and obligation is to pass on what I have discovered to be some of the most effective methods when managing students. It is my goal to add value to those that have the privilege and responsibility of managing students while transporting them or in any other environment where a child's safety and well-being is the number one priority.

Glenn P. Brooks, Jr.

ONE
Rules – Relationships = Rules

"Rules without Relationship leads to Rebellion" –Josh McDowell

It is widely understood to those that manage students, that if you're going to be effective it starts with developing a relationship with them. Think about it, when is the last time you blindly followed someone just because they said so? Not often correct? Why do you think that is? If your answer is along the lines of "Because I don't know them or I don't trust them or I'm not sure I even like this person" then welcome to the world of a student. They are not going to follow you simply because of who you are or the title that you have. People tend to follow you when they have a relationship with you. For all my "old school" friends who are still holding on to the logic that "I am the authority and the kids should do what I say because I said so." My question is - how's that working for you? I'm going to take a wild guess and say probably not so well huh?

You see the generation that we serve today is very different than the one many of us grew up in. Many of us were raised to understand that if an adult or an authority said to do something you just did it. You may not have liked it or agreed with it but you did it anyway. Having been involved in managing students in one capacity or another for half of my adult life and the one thing that I can say that has remained constant is CHANGE.

Students are constantly evolving, whether I agree with the changes or not is not what is most important. What is most important is that I as the "authority figure" must figure out how to connect to my students. By nature rules are made to govern, maintain order and create boundaries, but let me very clear here, although rules are ABSOLUTELY necessary they are not human. Rules cannot reason, they are not compassionate nor have the ability to give a student the benefit of the doubt. As a result they have to be administered with great care and responsibility.

For example I had a student, I will call him James. James was a student on a bus route that I inherited from another driver. The entire bus was full of middle school students from a pretty rough neighborhood. What the kids did not know was that I grew up in a neighborhood just like theirs. I uniquely understood the struggle of growing up poor, and being subjected to all that comes with that economic status. James was a little guy with a BIG MOUTH. I recognized him immediately, because he could have been me as a child. He was small, quick with words but with absolutely NO self-control. He had a bad habit of being loud and disruptive. One day I decided enough was enough. He had gotten up out of his seat while the bus was in motion and this was on the heels of me telling him to please turn around and sit down "back to back, bottom to bottom and book bag in your lap" which is a big rule we used in my county that helps to keep the students safe particularly in the event of an accident. I could have written him up on a referral which would have led him to being suspended off the bus. In this case, I decided to call his parents to attempt to enlist there support in the matter before I resorted to "writing him up." I am so glad I took the time to reach out to his folks. What I found out changed my entire perspective. James' mother shared with me that he had ridden a special needs bus during the previous school year because of his ADHD and behavioral problems. She also said that he was one referral away from being expelled from the school he was attending and sent to an alternative school for kids with behavior issues. At that point I realized that this young man was not behaving badly for no apparent reason, but due to internal factors. There were reasons why he was behaving this way. Knowing this made it personal for me, it also made me understand that this student needed to be worked with not just dealt with and that makes a difference.

Does this mean that you can ignore the behavior? No it does not. But knowing the bigger picture can help you gain insight as to how you may be able to influence your student to change his or her behavior for the better. Far too often as managers of students we find ourselves just dealing with the behavior which is the symptom and not dealing with the problem that causes the behavior.

As far as I was concerned this was a real simple fix. I reassigned his seat for the majority of the year. I sat him right behind me which enabled me to develop a relationship with him in order to get a better insight as to how he thought. So when he behaved this way again and he did I would know how to better deal with the behavior and influence him to redirect his actions thus giving me what I wanted and that was a student who was seated properly that I could transport safely. This is better known as a "WIN-WIN situation."

I remember telling his mother how his behavior was changing and she thanked me profusely she even told me "Christmas is about to come early for you, Mr. Glenn." I laughed at her gesture and I told her that was not necessary, but I really appreciated the thought.

This made me recognize that making a connection with students was the key to best managing their behavior. I also understood that if I made the effort and gave it my best shot to work with my students, in most cases it would turn out favorably. Students are people and people have stories. When a connection occurs that's when you can lead, and that is when you can start making a difference.

My entire goal for putting this little book together is to help others see the value in connecting with people and showing you with REAL stories how this can be done. Everyone is different, every story is different, what works for me may not always work for you, and what works for others may not always work for you. But what I have found to be true is that experience is a great teacher and it's very possible to learn through others experiences. This is where training and education for those in public service becomes invaluable.

TWO
It's all in a name

I made it a point to get to know the names of ALL of my students. My goal at the beginning of each school year was to learn all the names of each student on each of my four routes by the Thanksgiving break. School for us started the first week in August. This meant I had about three months to learn about one hundred and seventy-five names. The challenge was that during this time frame many students were still being added or taken off your routes for a bunch of reasons. Everything from moving in and out of neighborhoods, to being newly enrolled in school, to getting rides, and even driving themselves. To say that every day was different would be an understatement. However I knew that learning the names of every student would be one of my biggest and most effective tools to managing them well.

You see when you have a bunch of kids in one place and they all have different personalities, agendas, and maturity levels getting an individual students attention can be really tough. If you're not careful, you can lose your patience quick in these situations, and when that happens, things can go from bad to worse in a

"New York Minute." We have all seen the disturbing "Breaking News" reports that captures a parent, coach, educator, and sometimes a bus driver on camera who has obviously snapped while dealing with students. I believe those melt downs stem from something that took place long before that camera capturing moment. Granted there are times where things escalate beyond control very quickly, but in many cases there was a spark, something that ignited the event. If we as managers of students can seek to discover who our students are and how to connect with them, I believe most of the problems we face can be greatly reduced. There is no quicker way to getting a students' attention than to call their name OUT LOUD.

I'll never forget that spring afternoon while driving my middle school route home. My supervisor was on board that day performing our biyearly "check ride" which was a standard review procedure from someone on our leadership team which was done to ensure that we were observing the policies and procedures of the county. The supervisor was also there to give us any wisdom on how we could improve as a Bus Managers.

I had just dropped my third stop and was on my way to my last stop when a bee flew in the window. Now in Georgia it tends to get hot long before summer and this day was no different. All the windows where down and the kids where excited as usual and as we approached the last stop a bee flew on the bus. Bees and other flying insects often times will get on the bus and typically the students will go bananas at the mere sight of something like that. I was able to talk the remaining students down from becoming hysterical while the bee was flying around on the bus. Because I knew all of my students' names I was able to call them by name as I saw the bee approaching them. "Kim I need you to sit in your seat, Carla it's going to be okay." I continued calling them by name wherever the bee was and encouraged that student to remain calm. I was able to calmly share that I would get it off the bus as soon as we came to a stop. I managed this all this while navigating through the busy afternoon traffic and no one came unglued even though they were dipping and dodging every time the bee came near them. They were saying things like "Oh God it's going to sting me" but thankfully it worked out well and no one got stung. Once the final student was off the bus and my route was complete, my supervisor looked at me and shared that she had never seen that before. She reminded me that she had driven a bus for years before becoming a supervisor and she had never seen anybody talk their students down from going hysterical. They just kind of assumed that acting hysterical was what they were going to do and you would just hope for the best. She restated that she had just seen something she had never seen before - WOW!

I have to be honest – I had never seen anything quite like that either but I don't think that is because it had not happened before. Quite honestly

I have met a ton of teachers, mentors, coaches and bus drivers that have similar connections with their students. However, the common trait that we all seem to have is that we all have a strong desire to do whatever is necessary to connect with our students. Everything else usually follows.

THREE
Atta boy!

Relationship Connection Key #1: Affirmation

According to Webster's dictionary affirmation is defined as the confirmation or ratification of the truth or validity of a prior judgment, decision, etc.

In order to develop a relationship with a student there are certain building blocks that need to be established for a foundation in order to make that possible. The next several chapters will serve as a guide of what I refer to as "relationship connection keys" to building a relationship not based exclusively on rules.

Before we get started I want to make sure one thing is very clear. These relationship connection keys serve as a backdrop to building a relationship. These keys in and of themselves mean nothing if they are not used and motivated by a heart of compassion.

Picture these connection keys as a skeleton if you will. A skeleton is merely a collective of bones assembled together in such a way that provides a structure for the body to function properly. Without the muscle, the tissue, and vital organs like the heart and brain the skeleton is just a lifeless bag of bones. Dealing with your students without building a personal relationship and having an exclusively "rules-based" relationship will not equal a connection - it takes rules along with a personal relationship in order to make a connection.

It's going to be hard to forget one of my high school students, we will call him Tony. He was a kid that I picked up on my very first stop in the morning. For months he was the only student on that stop and he was always on time. My high school pick up time for Tony was at six twenty-five am and you could expect to see him there with his headphones on bobbing his head and dancing to a beat that only he could hear. What was funny was that he was not concerned about what people thought as they drove by on a busy street prior to me arriving to pick him up. The thing that was most surprising was that Tony would take his headphones off when sitting behind me and talk to me for the next few minutes until we got to the next stop.

The conversations started out about random stuff, like the weather or how he had a bunch of homework the night before and how he did not do it because he fell asleep. But as the days turned into weeks and the weeks turned into months our conversations begin getting a little deeper. Life conversations I call them. He would tell me about his childhood and how he had been in and out of juvenile detention centers. He shared with me that he had been kicked out of his last school and how now he was trying to figure it out and get his life together. He loved music and wanted to be a producer. He had a little makeshift studio and was trying to build it up so he could record at home instead of having to rent studio time. That opened up the door for me to talk to him about my days in radio and the fact that I did voice over work on the side. It turned out that we had a few things in common. Like myself this kid was from a single parent home. His mother was doing the best she could do to provide for her two boys, which even included her moving to this particular neighborhood because it was better than where they used to live. Ultimately her hope was that her boys would turn out to be somebody. How did I know this? Well that is because he talked about his mother and her expectations of them often.

I realized in these conversations that the more he talked the more I would listen and the more I realized he was looking for someone to affirm him. He wanted someone to confirm or validate the truth in what he was saying. He was looking to share his thoughts with someone that was not going to be so rules oriented or ridged. He did not need to always here statements like, this is what you're *"supposed"* to do or you *"need"* to do this or you "need" to do that. He needed affirmation and approval. This is where relationship connection key number one played a big part in our developing a relationship. Every time Tony would talk to me about an accomplishment he had made, whether it was pulling a failing grade up, or a new piece of equipment that he had installed for his recording studio, I would find myself telling him how much I knew he could do it because of the work he had put in to get there. He needed to hear more **"Atta boy"** statements like "I am proud of you and you should be proud of yourself."

I remember once when he was stressed out about trying to get a job because his mother could not afford to give him "things". He was applying for a job with a local fast food restaurant and he didn't have a clue as to what he should wear, how he should talk or what to even say on an interview. As I gave him tips and reminded him of how fearless and articulate he was, he meticulously would repeat the tips back to me and say "OK so if they say this I should say that?" We role played different interview scenarios on the bus in between stops. After filling out several applications he finally got the call to come in for an interview. As his interview date quickly approached we went back over all the things we had talked about and how to handle himself. Why the need to establish eye contact was so important. How to ask probing questions of the employer willing to hire you. After I dropped him off at home that day, as I drove off I said a little prayer for him hoping he would get the job. Sure enough that next morning he was dancing as usual but this time with a little bit more energy. As soon as I popped the door open he looked at me with a huge grin, nodded his head in affirmation as he walked up the steps past me and sat down. When he sat down I looked in the mirror and said well what happened? In his very cool monotone voice he said in his south west Atlanta accent and slang "You already know what it is Mr. Glenn - I got the job!!! Thanks for all your help." I was so excited for him I didn't know what to do but shake my head while grinning like I'd won the lottery or something. All the while telling him "you did it Buddy...you did it."

As the weeks and months went on he would tell me about the

different things he was experiencing at work on his new job. He would share with me the compliments he was getting and even how difficult it was to learn their process. As I think back and reflect, it is amazing that something as simple as him receiving an **"Atta boy"** helped him to find it within himself to keep pushing.

Our relationship started out with me being willing to ask questions, do a lot of listening, and affirm this young man as often as I could. As a result when he had momentary setbacks I was able to challenge him on the way he was thinking about things from a different perspective thus causing him to make decisions that he assisted him in learning to grow through things ant not run from things.

Everyone needs to be affirmed especially students. If you give them an ***"Atta boy"*** for legitimate accomplishments you'll find that when they have set backs it'll be easier to connect with them in order to help them.

FOUR
What you see is what you get

Relationship Connection Key #2: Acceptance
Acceptance is a favorable reception approval and or favor.

Having grown up in an era where kids were seen and not heard it took me a long time to understand the value of accepting things as they are and not how I want them to be. I am sure many readers who came from that old school mentality can relate to what I am saying. It took me having children of my own in a time that was nothing like when I grew up to really begin wrapping my mind around, that it is possible to accept them for who they are and not force them to change into what or who I wanted them to be. Children, students, kids whatever you want to call them, are also people. They have their own ideas, their own thoughts, their own identity and their own desires.

If I am honest there were times that I didn't want to manage my own children, I wanted to control them. In other words I was not looking to accept them as much as I wanted them to accept my way. Now I fully understand that connecting to them starts with accepting them.

We've all heard the statement "it is my way or the highway" Correct? Well the challenge with that is that when your job is to manage students' behavior day in and day out, that rigid thought process in most cases is not effective. This is especially true when dealing with older students. Accepting students involves you being willing to put your likes and desires aside for what they want. Let me give you an example - if you have ever ridden on a school bus with seventy elementary students you will quickly recognize that the word loud begins to take on a completely different meaning. It can get so loud that you literally cannot hear yourself think. Even though your students may be having regular conversation at a conversational tone, it can be extremely loud on an enclosed metal bus.

My preference would be that they would just be quiet, not say a word, and ride down the street like little angels and do exactly what I say (wishful thinking-huh). But my reality is that they've been in class all day long where they had to sit and be quiet; quite frankly they're excited to go home. My refusal to accept the truth that these are children, ages five to eleven, and the likelihood of them being completely quiet is slim to none. And if that is my goal everyday then I set myself up to become their adversary not their leader. If and when you become their enemy then all chances of connecting with them are gone. This does not mean that you have to be their friend. However, as the manager, you have to learn how to become an influencer. John Maxwell said it best when he made the statement "leadership is influence nothing more and nothing less".

As the bus manager my acceptance of who my students are helps me to connect to them so that I can get them to do what I need them to do. So in the case of a loud bus I oftentimes have to be creative regarding the method I use to get them to be quiet. My students knew the rules regarding noise levels on the bus because I had reviewed the bus rules with them routinely. However getting them to carry them out was another issue all together. For instance, I implemented doing something as simple as turning on the lights and instructing them that when the lights are on, their mouths are closed. This only works when you make sure that you only turn the lights on when it is absolutely needed. Another trick I learned from my field trainer was simply tapping on your microphone to create a thumping sound to get their attention. When everybody begins to listen and pay attention they will recognize that the lights are on. Then you can simply put up two fingers which is the non-verbal sign that means be quiet. Then you can say (although I would normally sang it with my elementary kids) "Put your fingers up-shh, shh… Put your fingers up shh-shh." At that point the sound level has gone down from a ten to a five. Then I am able to say: "Hey guys the lights are on and I need it quiet please." Whatever method or technique you use the goal is to demonstrate acceptance in order to reach the desired outcome on your bus.

This all reminds me of the time a student told me once "we can't be quiet Mr. Glenn it's not in our nature." Rather than get upset with this middle school student, even though she was right, I decided that it would be in all of our best interests for me to redefine what quiet meant. Up until then quiet for me was total silence. Now for me quiet is a level of which I can communicate to them and they can communicate to me without anybody yelling and screaming at each other.

To put it in a phrase I learned years ago when I was in the Army. I had to learn to **adjust, adapt and then overcome**.

FIVE
Give honor where it is due

Relationship Connection Key #3: Appreciation
Appreciation is simply showing gratitude.

In this next chapter I want to talk a little bit about how the idea of appreciation has everything to do with showing gratitude regularly.

In many cases most of us who manage students for a living can attest to the fact that often times some of our students are coming from families or backgrounds that are not particularly favorable. Some of them are growing up in single parent homes, no parent homes, foster homes, group homes and the list can continue. However for the small amount of time that we have them in our care I have found that the more I can appreciate, be thankful, recognize them, or show gratitude towards them it becomes so much easier for me to manage them.

I heard a coworker once say that it doesn't cost anything to smile. It never ceases to amaze me how something as simple as a smile can change the mood and attitude of a student. I made it a habit to tell myself before I even picked up my first student each day that "it is game time." Meaning it's time to go to work and be the best me possible.

Let's face it, as educators, leaders, mentors, and the likes we all are human first. As a result we don't always feel like smiling or saying good morning. Perhaps you have been up all night with a sick child, had an argument with your spouse or are not getting along with a coworker. Whatever the issue the truth of the matter is that sometimes you have to motivate yourself just to be able to give the students what they need, which is your very best. It's the leader's job to go first. If you want appreciation, if you want gratitude, if you want thankfulness practice giving it first. I took the time to develop the habit, notice that I said a habit, which simply means I made a conscious effort to remember my students' names and say good morning to them EVERY single day. This sounds so simple but you would be surprised how many people don't appreciate, understand or practice smiling and saying good morning and calling someone's name.

I remember that it was the middle of the school year when I got one particular new student on my bus. She was from another country and didn't speak English very well at all. We will call her Antoinette, I made it a point to say good morning to her in her native language and call her by her name every day. Sometimes she would respond with a nod, and sometimes she would say hello. As the year went on I had not recognized that her English was getting better because she never talked very much. To my surprise when I announced that I would not be returning the next school year several of my students gave me cards expressing their gratitude towards me. Antoinette wrote "Thank you Mr. Glenn for speaking to me every day and always calling me by my name. Although you are my very first bus driver you are the best bus driver that I've ever had and I'm so sorry to see you go. I wish you well. You are the best." She wrote this in perfect English and it brought me to tears because I never recognized that the little act of saying hello in one of my students' language every day and calling their name would make such an impact.

I try to approach managing students from a balanced perspective; as much as you may need to discipline, it is equally as important to reward them when they do something right. This will show them that they are appreciated. Nothing reminds me more of this than the middle school route that I picked up partially through the school year. The students on this route had become particularly difficult to deal with for their previous driver. Things were so bad with this route that during the previous school year the assistant principal had to ride the bus in order to identify the troublemakers and help the bus manager make adjustments.

The behavior of the students on this route had gotten completely out of control. The girls were beating up boys, and there were incidents of students jumping out of windows at the bus stop among other things. The students often left the bus full of trash as they exited. The minute I took over this route there was one thing I realized had to happen immediately and that was that I need to make a connection with these students quickly in order to maintain any level of order. One of the things that I instituted immediately was that if they could keep the bus clean and trash free every week I would give them a treat at the end of each week. This worked so well that after six or seven straight weeks of a clean bus I decided to throw them a pizza party. When the school administration informed me that for logistical reasons I could not throw the party a backup plan was needed. With my supervisors permission I put together a plan to give them treats (big bags of Takis, a popular chip which was the treat of choice for my students) as each student exited the bus. The students were blown away that I would spend my own money to reward them for weeks of excellent behavior. This simple act of gratitude resulted in my rarely having any more trash on my bus for the remainder of the school year and only having to write two referrals. This was not because I was special and it was not because I did anything that others could not do. The fact that I actually executed on an idea to show gratitude made the difference. I learned from that experience to always *give honor where honor is due.* It will reap huge dividends on the back end.

SIX
Perception is reality

Relationship Connection Key #4: Approachable

Be accessible – easy to meet, know, talk, etc...

As we continue to talk about what it takes to build solid relationships with students in order to manage them properly this next relationship connection key is absolutely vital. If you're not approachable and what I mean by that is if you're not capable of being accessible or easy to talk to, it is going be very tough for you to be able to develop relationships with not only your students but anyone else that you have to interact with on a regular basis.

Most people would say that they are approachable, but if you were to ask ten people who know you the best what do you think they would say? Would they say the same?

There are a few ways that you can tell whether or not you are approachable. Do people tend to tell you what is on their mind? Perhaps people regularly seek your opinion? Or maybe people say things like "you are so easy to talk to." If these things are true of you then that probably means you are approachable.

However if the opposite is true, meaning you notice that people get quiet when you come around. Or perhaps you find yourself using the statements like "you know you can tell me anything right" in order to remind them that you are approachable. This may mean that you have some work to do in the area of being truly approachable. Trust me I know that this does not come easy to everyone. You may love students but you are really an introvert. I just want to encourage you to do your best to grow in that area and come outside of your comfort zone.

In order to manage students or to manage people in general they have to want to be around you. I remember growing up and my mother would often have a very serious look on her face that was somewhat intimidating. I found myself constantly asking her "are you okay?" or "did I do something wrong?" Keep in mind I was the child who was always doing something that I was not supposed to be doing. Her response would often be "No son there is nothing wrong, why do you ask?" I did not have the courage to tell her what I really was thinking. So I would just shrug my shoulders as if to say I did not know. In reality what I was really thinking was that something had to be wrong because her face was scrunched up like a prune.

If your body language, your posture, or your facial expressions communicate that you do not want to be bothered - trust me your students will not approach you. However if you can learn to smile on purpose, engage them, establish eye contact and talk to them and not at them then you will show that you are approachable.

They will at least feel like they can bring something to you when it is necessary. All you can hope for is that when the time arises and you are needed by your students, that they feel like they can come to you and share. All bus managers know and understand that before you drive your bus it must be pre-tripped. That simply means go through and check it to make sure that it is serviceable, that it functions properly and that it is safe to drive. Well I have learned to also pre- trip myself to make sure my attitude is right, and that I am not wearing my problems on my face or scrunching it like a prune so that I can be up to the task of managing my students.

SEVEN
Caring starts with us

Relationship Connection Key #5: Attentive

Attentive is defined as thinking about and paying close attention to something, as well as being very concerned about the needs of others according to Meriam -Webster dictionary.

This next relationship connection key has to do with what I believe to be the center of what it takes to be able to manage students well and that is...you must be attentive. You will notice that the definition of this word speaks to giving attention to or being observant.

When this connection key is used properly on the front end it will save you a bunch of drama on the back end. Before we get started let me say that I think that it is absolutely essential for a person who is going to manage students for a living to have a genuine care for students. You must have a genuine love and passion for students. If not, the concepts referred to in these relationship connection keys will seem foreign to you. The implementation will feel unnatural and mechanical and your students will sense your uneasiness. Many professionals can attest to this fact. Children know when you're faking it. They know when you don't like them or you don't care about them. When you are attentive to your students that is when they know you care, but if at your core you do not like children, managing them may not be the profession for you.

I remember one instance on my middle school route when I had a new student who I observed to be a bit of a jokester. I also noticed that everyone in the back of the bus seemed to follow her lead. I did not say anything at first as I normally make it a habit to observe people for a while to get a read on who they are before making any judgment. However something did not sit right with me concerning this young lady.

One day as we were going to school I noticed the bus was particularly loud that morning with kids laughing and joking around. As I sat back and watched it seemed as if the new student was the center of all the commotion. So once we arrived to the school and the other students were unloading I asked her to stay behind. Once the other students were off the bus I asked her what was all the joking about and she immediately began to get defensive. That is when I calmly let her know about some of the rules of our bus. I told her that I did not mind them having fun but that they could not be unsafe. What I meant by unsafe was them being turned around, up and out of their seat, that sort of thing. She seemed to understand the rules and it appeared that this would be the end of her leading the disruption on the bus.

Needless to say it happened again. The students were getting so loud that they were becoming a distraction to me. At the center of the commotion was this new student. I resorted to moving her seat and having her sit up close to me. She complied but was clearly in shock that I had disciplined her for leading the commotion. Over the next few days I began to engage her in conversation. We would talk about stuff like what she wanted to be and the kind of things that it would take for her to accomplish her goals. I could tell she was definitely a leader and we connected. Over time she grew to understand that I was not getting on the students for no reason, but that I was generally concerned for their safety. With this new understanding I was able to move her back to her original seat with her now being my ally and I had very few problems from her.

The point is that when you slow down and take the time to pay attention to your students it will help you to deal with the real issue rather than rushing to judgment based on your assumptions. This also allows you to give the benefit of doubt to those students who you know are typically obedient and respectful. When you are respectful and polite people will generally respect you for it and allow you to lead them. This takes work, but the work is a little easier when they know you care.

EIGHT
See what you see

Relationship Connection Key #6:
Aware
Be informed, alert, and knowledgeable about your students.

As an educational professional the truth is you are not going to catch everything! We are not going to be on top of every single thing. Years ago I had the opportunity and pleasure to meet and befriend the publisher of a very popular magazine. We were talking about the subject of determination and she made a statement that I will never forget.

She shared with me that throughout her professional development she had come to the conclusion that there was nothing more powerful than "a made up mind." When you make up your mind that you are going to do your best to be aware by practicing being conscious, being alert, being knowledgeable, and being informed of what's going on with your students, there will not be much that will get by you.

As a teacher you may notice that you have a student in your classroom that has been wearing the same clothes every day to school. At that point perhaps you discover that they are homeless or for whatever reason mom or dad are unable to wash their clothes. Noticing things like this helps you not only understand the students home situation but also gives you an idea of what type of support the student may need to help them succeed socially and academically in school.

As a daycare provider you may notice that Mom and Dad are arguing in the car prior to dropping off Lil Johnny, so if Lil Johnny has an attitude all day or he is feeling angry, upset or embarrassed, you have a great indication as to why. Once again paying attention to the little things oftentimes will give you a leg up on what's going on with the students' behavior.

I had a kindergartener once, we will call him Nick, who was oftentimes not being met at his bus stop. Nick had an older sister that road my high school bus who would meet him at the bus stop until she began running track. The policy in the county that I drove for was that either a parent, an older sibling, or a pre-approved designated person was required to pick up all kindergartners at the bus stop every day. When his sister started running track for the high school track team their mother starting coming to pick up Nick. It was not long before I noticed that mom was coming to the bust stop later and later to pick him up. Sometimes she would not show up at all which resulted in me having to take him back to school in order for her to come pick him up there. After this happened the third time I decided to put a phone call into her to see if there was anything wrong and if there was anything I could do to help. She shared with me that her job had changed her shift and that she had to do some training which was causing her to run a little late. It turned out that he was the last stop of this route, so I was able to give her a few minutes to show up before taking him back to the school.

Now I did not have to make a concession for this mom, but because I was aware of what was going on I was able to make an adjustment that benefited my student and parent. I am certain that this simple act took some stress off of her and her son as well. The way I see it is my job is to go above and beyond whenever possible if it will benefit my students. My goal was to make a connection not just with the student but the parents as well.

I am sure many of you who are reading this have experienced the pleasure of going above and beyond the scope of your job. Trust me that does not go unnoticed. Remember your students feel the love every time you show that level of care.

NINE
Always be there

Relationship Connection Key #7: Available

Being available is being readily accessible

One of the things that I absolutely love about managing students is that every day is always different. Sometimes it is the first day of the school year, sometimes it is the last, or perhaps it is a test day. Whatever day it is, each day brings about its own challenges.

I encourage you to put all of these relationship connection keys to work. *Affirm* your students and learn to *accept* them for who they are not for just what they do. *Appreciate* them as much as you can while being *approachable*. Always stay alert and pay *attention*. To the best of your ability make sure that you're *aware* of what is going on with your students. Lastly you want to make it a habit to be *available* to them.

I know it is literally impossible to be available to each and every student one hundred percent of the time. However what is very possible almost one hundred percent of the time is to use the resources that you have at your disposal to give your students the feeling that you're always there for them.

Perhaps you have some free time and you chose to give it as a mentor at one of the schools or the places that you come in contact with your students. It has always amazed me how when you give just a little bit of time it makes so much difference in their lives.

This brings to mind some of the student athletes that rode my bus. These guys were so competitive and I would often overhear them talking about what they did in the game last night, who scored what and who did not score. One day I decided to announce to the bus that I was going to be at the next game so that we could really talk about who did what. If nothing else it would keep those "fish tales" in check. Boy did that create a buzz. Everyone on the bus that day was talking about my coming to the game and many of them even challenged me by making statements like "Mr. Glenn you're not going to come out" or "Yeah right, you won't show up, whatever!" So you can imagine their surprise when I actually showed up at the game. My students who were not on the playing field and were seated in the stands were just as surprised. I must admit that there are not many feelings greater than having a student scream your name from across the bleachers. I got the chance to hang out with some of my students and meet their parents, siblings, aunts, uncles, cousins, and friends. You see in the south they take their sports very, very serious it's like a religion or something.

I had not done anything grandiose, but to my students it meant the world. Just like you I care and I just gave what little I had, and that was simply my time. For you that could be simply showing up to the school to treat some of your students to lunch for making honor roll. You will be amazed at how much it can brighten up a students' day when you invest in their lives. Being available also means listening to a student tell you about their day, especially when they are in kindergarten or first grade and you are the first person they see when they get out of school. Just thinking about those moments will always make my heart happy.

My hope is that after reading this book you will be encouraged to dig deep and do something different. Go ahead think outside of the box, take an idea that I have shared to the next level and make an intentional connection with your students. Take these relationship connection keys that I have laid out and make them your own. Change them around, add to some or take away from some. Whatever you do make a difference, make a connection and make the commitment to *manage your students through relationships not rules.*

Notes

Acknowledgments

To my best friend, wife and partner Sheri Brooks. Sweetheart thanks for your patience and pleasantly pushing me to always be who God created me to be and never quit.

To all of my colleagues over the past twenty-five years who've helped me grow in my ability to connect and add value to others. Your input and wisdom continues to serve so many.

To Sandra Leon, Terrence Haymon, and Jane Stovall thanks for being the best trainers and instructors EVER. Your commitment to excellence always challenged me to do my best.

To Joyce Kennedy and Penny Macenczak for your true commitment to your staff. You made us all feel special.

To Patty Chronic, Chris Ewing, Becky Hart and Elliot Perkins you guys are relentless in your support of all your bus managers.

There was never a day that I didn't feel empowered to do my job.

To all of my fellow 062 and 038 drivers. You guys set the standard for what it looks like to show up every day, on time, with a servants heart and a desire to do right by our students. If you ever wonder how awesome you are just think about the snow storm of 2014. No child was left behind.

About the author

Glenn P. Brooks, Jr, is a 20+ year veteran public speaker with experience working with numerous social service agencies, public school systems, and non-profits organizations in the Atlanta, GA, Richmond, VA, Washington, DC, and Baltimore, MD metropolitan areas as a speaker, workshop facilitator, mentor, and coach working with youth, parents, and leaders.

Glenn has worked directly with the state of Virginia's Family and Fatherhood Initiative speaking on parenting issues relevant to single mothers. He also developed and facilitated The Art of Public Speaking training program for the Staff Development Instructors of the Safety and Training Division for Gwinnett County Public Schools Transportation in Georgia, which provides novice and experienced public speakers with the foundational tools needed to connect with their audience. He currently serves as an outside consultant with the Pupil Transportation Safety Institute (PTSI) providing training for transportation professionals.

Glenn is a published author of the following titled releases: How To Raise A Man... Not A Momma's Boy, Living With A Momma's Boy, and How I Got My Son Back which deal with parenting issues.

As the co-founder of Glenn P. Brooks, Jr. LLC. and Constant Relationship Coaching which were founded in 2012. Glenn's mission is to equip people with the tools to communicate, connect, and consider others in order to build and maintain healthy relationships in their personal and professional lives.

Glenn is an Army veteran, father, grandfather, and husband who has always had a passion to make a real impact in the lives of students and parents. He is a firm believer that John Maxwell was correct when he stated that "Leadership is influence - nothing more - nothing less". It is his life's purpose to influence others to be the best leaders possible in their homes and businesses.

To book Glenn P. Brooks, Jr. as a speaker, workshop facilitator, or consultant for your organization visit www.GlennPBrooksJr.com or contact him at Glenn@GlennPBrooksJr.com.

Made in the USA
Lexington, KY
10 June 2018